FREEDOM'S PROMISE

# THE FREEDMEN'S BUREAU

BY DUCHESS HARRIS, JD, PHD
WITH BONNIE HINMAN

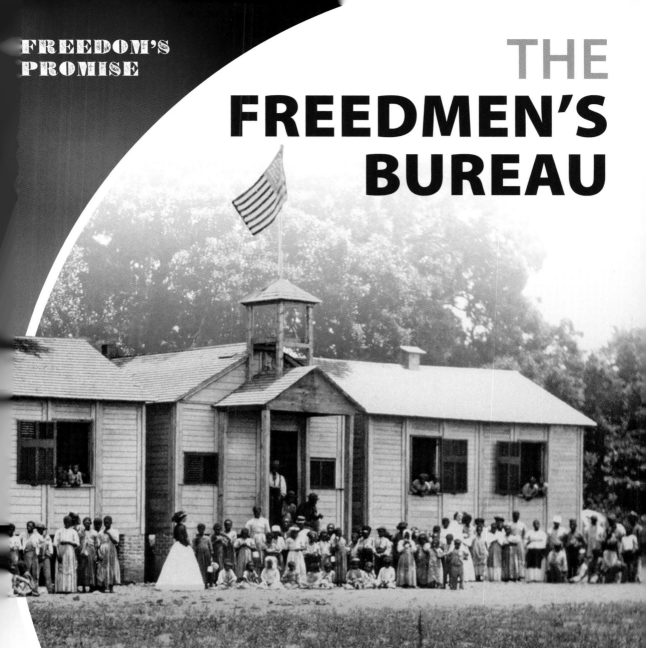

Cover image: The Freedmen's Bureau helped build many schools for African Americans.

Core Library
An Imprint of Abdo Publishing
abdobooks.com

abdocorelibrary.com

Published by Abdo Publishing, a division of ABDO, PO Box 398166, Minneapolis, Minnesota 55439. 

Printed in the United States of America, North Mankato, Minnesota
032019
092019

THIS BOOK CONTAINS RECYCLED MATERIALS

Cover Photo: Corbis Historical/Getty Images
Interior Photos: Corbis Historical/Getty Images, 1; North Wind Picture Archives, 5, 17, 30–31, 36–37; Metropolitan Museum of Art, NY/Newscom, 6–7; Everett Historical/Shutterstock Images, 10, 19, 43; Red Line Editorial, 12, 41; World History Archive/Newscom, 14–15; Ben Shahn NC History Images/Newscom, 22–23; Picture History/Newscom, 25; Maryann Groves/North Wind Picture Archives, 27; World History Archive/Alamy, 40

Editor: Maddie Spalding
Series Designer: Claire Vanden Branden

Library of Congress Control Number: 2018965960

Publisher's Cataloging-in-Publication Data

Names: Harris, Duchess, author | Hinman, Bonnie, author.
Title: The freedmen's bureau / by Duchess Harris and Bonnie Hinman
Description: Minneapolis, Minnesota: Abdo Publishing, 2020 | Series: Freedom's promise | Includes online resources and index.
Identifiers: ISBN 9781532118739 (lib. bdg.) | ISBN 9781532172915 (ebook)
Subjects: LCSH: United States. Bureau of Refugees, Freedmen, and Abandoned Lands--Juvenile literature. | African Americans--Social conditions--Juvenile literature. | Reconstruction (United States : 1865-1877)--Juvenile literature. | United States--Race relations--Juvenile literature.
Classification: DDC 973.714--dc23

# CONTENTS

# A LETTER FROM DUCHESS

After the Civil War ended in 1865, enslaved people were freed. They needed support and aid in this transition period. The Freedmen's Bureau was created for this purpose. The bureau is credited with helping formerly enslaved Black people set up schools and churches in the South. It also gave Black people supplies and medical aid.

A freedom that many people take for granted is the freedom to live with family. During the period of slavery, enslaved people had been separated from their family members. The bureau reunited formerly enslaved people with their families. But some people think it did not do enough to help Black people. The bureau did not have enough resources to provide aid to everyone. It faced a lot of opposition in the South.

I hope this book helps you think about what is needed to reconstruct a community. Join me on this journey to learn about the Freedmen's Bureau and its legacy.

Duchess Harris

Freedmen's Bureau workers spoke to freed slaves throughout the South.

# CHAPTER ONE

# REBUILDING THE SOUTH

The road south out of Atlanta, Georgia, was crowded on November 15, 1864. William T. Sherman and 62,000 of his troops were on the march. Sherman was a Union general. The American Civil War (1861–1865) had been going on for more than three years. The Union army fought for the North. Their opponent was the Confederate army. The Confederate army fought for the South. Sherman's forces had captured Atlanta from Confederate troops. They were headed for Savannah, Georgia. Savannah is on the East Coast by the Atlantic Ocean. This operation was called Sherman's March to the Sea.

**Some enslaved people escaped their slaveholders as Union troops swept through the South in 1864.**

## WHAT CAUSED THE CIVIL WAR?

**In the mid-1800s, the South's economy depended on slave labor. Each state decided whether to allow slavery within its borders. Many southerners defended states' rights. They didn't think the federal government should have the power to abolish slavery in states where it already existed. Many southerners hoped to expand slavery westward into new states. The new Republican Party opposed this expansion. Abraham Lincoln won the presidential election in 1860. Lincoln was a Republican. Many southerners feared that he would end slavery in the South. Eleven southern states seceded, or separated, from the United States. They formed the Confederate States of America, or the Confederacy. This disagreement led to the Civil War.**

Sherman's troops would move north after capturing Savannah. They would join Union general Ulysses S. Grant's troops. Then they would attack Confederate general Robert E. Lee's troops.

Thousands of black men, women, and children followed the soldiers. They were freed slaves. Earlier in the war, President Abraham Lincoln had signed the Emancipation Proclamation. This order said that all enslaved people in Confederate states would be free as of January 1, 1863. In reality, they only became free when Union troops arrived to enforce the order.

## MARCH TO THE SEA

Many enslaved people fled from their slaveholders as Union forces swept through the South. They were not sure slaveholders would obey the Emancipation Proclamation. They thought they would be safer with the Union army. They packed up their clothes. They followed Union troops across the South. Each day, the number of freed slaves following Union troops increased. Approximately 10,000 freed people traveled with Sherman's troops on the March to the Sea.

Sherman did not think the refugees were his responsibility. His main focus was destroying the Confederate army's resources. His troops destroyed tunnels, bridges, and railroads in Georgia. They burned plantations and fields. They took all the food they

Union troops burned and destroyed Confederate army resources during Sherman's March to the Sea.

could find. Sherman hoped this strategy would convince Confederate leaders to surrender.

Sherman arrived in Savannah in December 1864. By then the war was almost over. Lee surrendered in April 1865. His surrender ended the war. Former Confederate states rejoined the Union.

## CREATING THE BUREAU

By 1865 millions of people had escaped slavery or been freed. But many of them were homeless. They were also hungry and sick. In March 1865, the US Congress created the Bureau of Refugees, Freedmen, and Abandoned Lands. This agency was also known as the

Freedmen's Bureau. Its goal was to care for freed people and other war refugees.

The Thirteenth Amendment was ratified on December 6, 1865. This amendment abolished slavery. The Freedmen's Bureau gave former slaves aid and support as they started their new lives. Congress believed that the agency would only need to provide aid for a short time. Many people thought that the South would recover within one year.

## PERSPECTIVES

### RACISM IN THE SOUTH

**Many southerners hoped the Freedmen's Bureau would make freed people return to work on plantations. Southerners blamed the bureau officials when that did not happen. One Virginian wrote an angry letter to President Andrew Johnson. She said that her town was overrun with former slaves. She called them lazy. She referred to them as "negros." This word was common at the time but is considered offensive today. The woman wrote, "You are a southern man, sir, and well know what is absolutely necessary for a negro—they cannot be left to run wild."**

## BLACK POPULATION IN THE 1800s

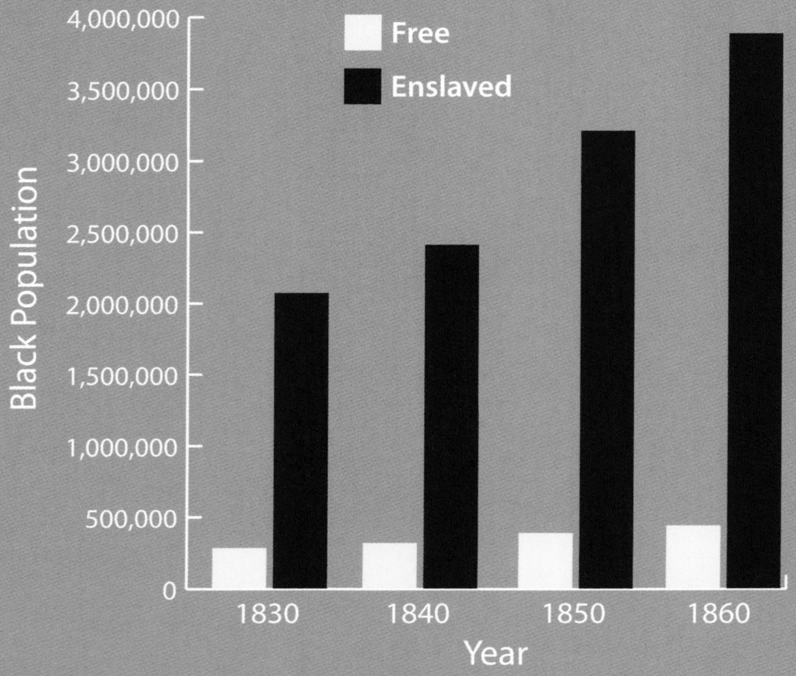


The above graph shows the population of freed black people in the United States before the Civil War. It also shows the population of enslaved black people in these years. Why do you think both populations rose in this time period? Does this graph help you understand how widespread slavery was?

Then southern states would be able to take care of their own residents. This proved to be wrong. The war was over, but many problems arose in its aftermath.

# STRAIGHT TO THE SOURCE

**W. E. B. Du Bois was an African American author and activist. In a magazine article, he explained why the Freedmen's Bureau was created. He wrote:**

> *The problem of the twentieth century is the problem of the color line; the relation of the darker to the lighter races of men in Asia and Africa, in America and the islands of the sea. It was a phase of this problem that caused the Civil War. . . . No sooner had Northern armies touched Southern soil than this old question, newly guised, sprang from the earth,—What shall be done with slaves? . . . At last there arose in the South a government of men called the Freedmen's Bureau . . . which sought to settle the Negro problems in the United States of America.*

Source: W. E. B. Du Bois. "The Freedmen's Bureau." *Atlantic Monthly*. Atlantic Monthly, March 1901. Web. Accessed October 15, 2018.

## Consider Your Audience

**Adapt this passage for a different audience, such as your friends. Write a blog post conveying this same information for the new audience. How does your post differ from the original text and why?**

*CHAPTER*
# TWO

# RECONSTRUCTION BEGINS

After the Thirteenth Amendment was ratified, the South had to adjust to the end of slavery. Southern states had relied on slavery. It provided a source of free labor. President Andrew Johnson tried to help the South through this transition period. His plan to help the South recover was called Presidential Reconstruction.

One of the first acts of Presidential Reconstruction was the formation of the Freedmen's Bureau. In May 1865, Johnson appointed Oliver Otis Howard commissioner of the bureau. Howard was a former Union general. He appointed assistant commissioners

**Freedmen's Bureau agents gave food and other aid to black refugees.**

## NEW FREEDOMS

**Former slaves used their new freedom in many ways. Some moved away from the places where they had been enslaved. Many enslaved families had been split up. Family members had been sold to different slaveholders. The Freedmen's Bureau helped former slaves find each other. The bureau provided transportation to help people search for their family members. It also helped former slaves get legally married. Marriage between enslaved people had not been recognized by law. After slavery ended, freed people wanted to make their marriages legal. Some bureau employees performed marriage ceremonies. Others issued marriage certificates.**

for each of the former Confederate states. These men hired assistants and local agents. The commissioners and their assistants made the rules for the bureau. The agents gave refugees food and clothing. They opened schools to educate black people. They helped refugees find jobs. They reported their efforts and progress to the commissioners.

Soldiers filled many positions in

**Oliver Otis Howard was commissioner of the Freedmen's Bureau from 1865 to 1872.**

the bureau. The US Army paid them. During the Civil War, many southerners fled their homes to escape approaching Union troops. The government seized much of this land after the war. The government allowed the bureau to sell or rent these lands. This helped pay for the bureau's activities.

## PROVIDING AID

Nearly 4 million freed slaves lived in the South after the Civil War. Many of them could not find jobs. They had little or no money. The Freedmen's Bureau fed thousands of them. The US Army supplied the bureau with food. The bureau also fed white refugees. These refugees were southerners who had been loyal to the Union. Confederate soldiers had chased them out of their homes.

The bureau also helped black soldiers and their families. Many freed slaves had fought in the Union army. The US government owed them payments for their service. The bureau helped black soldiers collect these payments. Widows of soldiers who had died during the war needed assistance too. The bureau helped them collect the payments their husbands had earned.

The bureau was soon feeding 148,120 people each day. Clothing came from former Confederate supplies and the US Army. Northern relief organizations also donated clothing to the bureau. Howard planned to decrease this aid after a few months. Congress believed

**Entire families had been enslaved and needed aid after the Civil War.**

refugees would not be motivated to search for jobs if relief was available.

## FINDING WORK

Black people had to find jobs to support themselves and their families. There was plenty of work to be done in the South. The South had lost many workers. Nearly 260,000 southerners had died in the war.

## PERSPECTIVES

### PRESIDENT ANDREW JOHNSON

**Andrew Johnson became president after Lincoln was assassinated in 1865. Johnson belonged to the Republican Party. His fellow Republicans hoped he would punish the South for seceding. Many northerners were Republicans. They did not think the government should give Confederate lands back to their former owners. They hoped Johnson would arrest some former Confederates. Instead, Johnson forgave almost all former Confederates. He gave back much of their property. He was against giving former slaves the right to vote. His actions disappointed many Republicans.**

Another 194,000 had been wounded in battle. Crops needed to be planted and harvested. Buildings needed repairs. Former slaves knew how to do these jobs. But most southerners did not want to hire former slaves. Many black people wanted to have their own farmland. They did not want to go back to work for planters.

## RIGHT TO LAND

Former slaves had good reason to think they would get land.

Congress said that the Freedmen's Bureau could rent up to 40 acres (16 ha) of abandoned land to each freed person in the South. The person could farm the land for three years while paying rent. Any money earned from the crops would belong to whoever lived on the land. The occupant would be allowed to buy and own the land after three years.

Howard began to rent land to freed people. But Johnson had second thoughts about this plan. He decided that the original owners should get their land back. The bureau even took back land that had already been rented to freed people.

## FURTHER EVIDENCE

**Chapter Two describes some of the work that the Freedmen's Bureau did. What is one of the main points of this chapter? What evidence is included to support this point? Read the article at the website below. Does the information on the website support this point? Does it present new evidence?**

FREEDMEN'S BUREAU
**abdocorelibrary.com/freedmens-bureau**

*CHAPTER*
# THREE

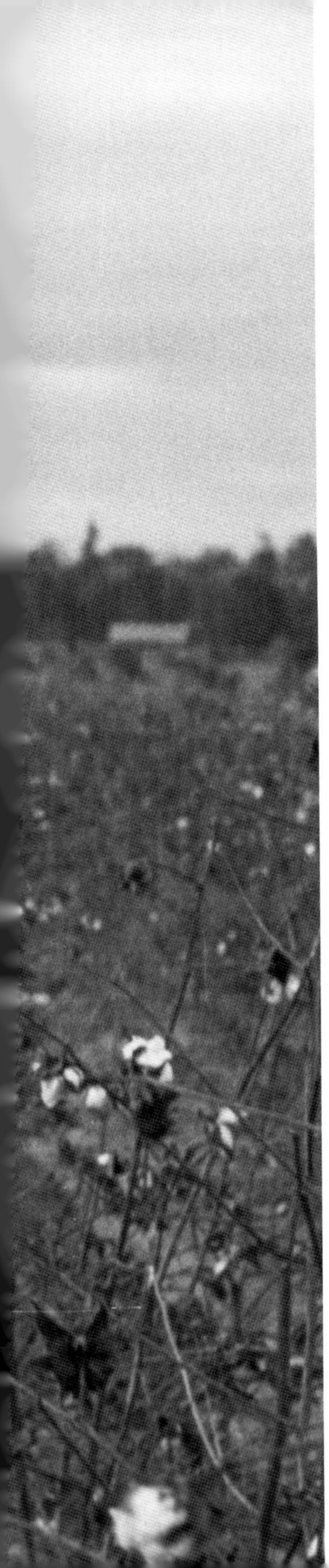

# THE BUREAU'S EARLY WORK

Employment was scarce for freed people. White people did not give them many job opportunities. Many black southerners went back to working on plantations. They did not have much choice. They became sharecroppers. Sharecroppers rented small plots of land from white landowners. They grew and harvested crops on the land. They had to give some of their crop to the landowners. They had to buy equipment, food, and other items from the landowners. Because of all these expenses, sharecroppers often ended up in debt.

**With few opportunities available, many black people became sharecroppers in the South after the Civil War.**

## PERSPECTIVES

### SUGAR PLANTERS RESIST

**Planters who owned sugar plantations thought free labor would not work. Free labor is a system where workers earn wages. They are free to choose their employment. Sugarcane had to be harvested on a specific schedule. The crop might fail if that schedule was not followed. Planters said that free labor would not work with sugar production. They believed that black people would only work when forced to do so. The planters did not think black people could be trusted to keep on schedule. Planters wanted the same kind of control they had over their slaves.**

The Freedmen's Bureau helped freed people find work. Bureau employees reviewed workers' labor contracts. Labor contracts said how much workers were to be paid and when. The contracts described the working conditions. Bureau employees made sure contracts were fair to workers. Overseeing labor contracts became the bureau's biggest job. Workers went

**Many black people fled the South in the late 1800s to escape violence and discrimination.**

to the bureau to file a complaint if their employers mistreated them.

## THE BLACK CODES

Johnson allowed southern lawmakers to create laws with little oversight. In 1865 and 1866, these lawmakers created new laws called the black codes. The black codes restricted the rights of black southerners. In some southern states, black people were not allowed to hold certain jobs. Black people who could not find work were punished for being unemployed. They were arrested or forced to pay a fine. If they could not pay the fine, law enforcement hired them out to companies. Companies forced them to work for no pay. The profits they made went to the companies. Many black convicts were forced to do hard labor, such as railroad construction. Black people who broke labor contracts could also be forced to do unpaid labor.

## EXTENDING THE BUREAU

The Freedmen's Bureau was supposed to exist for only one year after the end of the war. That would have been until May 1866. But officials soon saw that a year was not long enough. Black people still needed aid and support.

Congress proposed a new Freedmen's Bureau bill in February 1866. The bill would make the bureau a permanent government department. Johnson vetoed the bill. He thought the federal government should no longer provide aid to freed people. He believed the states should provide this aid.

**President Andrew Johnson wanted to end the Freedmen's Bureau in 1866.**

Congress made some changes to the bill. Members hoped these changes would make the bill more favorable to the president. Congress introduced this updated bill in July 1866. Johnson vetoed this bill too. But Congress passed it over his veto. The new bill said that the bureau could work until July 1868. It authorized the sale of some lands to freed people. Congress also voted to give federal funding to the bureau.

In April 1866, Congress passed the Civil Rights Act. This act protected the rights of freed people. It said that all people born in the United States were US citizens. Citizens have certain rights. They can own property and make contracts. They can bring cases to court and be protected by federal law. Lawmakers who passed this act were responding to injustices in the South. The act helped end the black codes.

## FREEDMEN'S BUREAU COURTS

**The second Freedmen's Bureau Act allowed the bureau to set up its own courts. In these courts, bureau employees settled disputes between black workers and white employers. In some cases, bureau agents decided the verdicts. The bureau also used three-man panels to decide cases. One of the panel members represented the black worker. Another member represented the white employer. The third member was the local bureau official. Both sides presented evidence. The panel decided a person's guilt or innocence.**

# STRAIGHT TO THE SOURCE

Many freed people wanted to be able to own their own land. Bayley Wyat was a black man from Virginia. He gave a speech explaining his views on black land ownership rights:

> *We [have] a right to the land where we are located. For why? I tell you. Our wives, our children, our husbands, has been sold over and over again to purchase the lands we now locates upon: for that reason we have a divine right to the land. . . . And then didn't we clear the land, and raise the crops of corn, of cotton, of tobacco, of rice, of sugar, of everything. And then didn't them large cities in the North grow up on the cotton and the sugars and the rice that we made? . . . I say they has grown rich, and my people is poor.*

Source: Eric Foner. *Reconstruction: America's Unfinished Revolution, 1863–1877*. New York: Harper & Row, 1988. Print. 105.

### Back It Up

Wyat used evidence to support his point. Write a paragraph describing the point he was making. Then write two or three pieces of evidence he used to make his point.

# CHAPTER FOUR

# HOSPITALS AND SCHOOLS

Employment was a major concern for freed people. Another concern was health care. The Freedmen's Bureau provided free health care to former slaves and poor white people. The bureau hired doctors. By November 1865, more than 80 bureau hospitals and clinics had been established. But more resources were needed to help all the people who needed health care. The federal government did not give the bureau enough funding to open more health-care facilities.

The bureau's hospitals and clinics were meant to be a temporary fix. The federal

**Black refugees formed settlements in the South in the late 1860s. The Freedmen's Bureau gave them health care and other aid.**

## PERSPECTIVES

### BUREAU COLLEGES

The Freedmen's Bureau founded colleges to train black teachers. Howard University is among the most well known of these colleges. Howard was founded in 1867 in Washington, DC. It was named after Freedmen's Bureau commissioner Oliver Otis Howard. The bureau also helped found Fisk University in Nashville, Tennessee. Activists W. E. B. Du Bois and Ida B. Wells both attended Fisk. Du Bois studied there in the late 1880s. He wrote: "I can hardly realize they are all my people; that this great assembly of youth and intelligence are representatives of a race which twenty years ago was in bondage."

government expected communities to run their own hospitals within a year. But many white southerners opposed this idea. They did not want to provide health care to former slaves. They did not want to be treated in the same hospitals as black people. Despite these problems, bureau officials shut down some hospitals. The bureau could not afford to keep them open any longer.

## EMERGENCY AID

Although the bureau's resources were limited, bureau workers still treated people. They provided aid in emergencies. Many freed people lived in crowded places where disease could spread quickly. Outbreaks of deadly diseases hit parts of the South in the 1860s. In April 1867, a cholera outbreak hit Helena, Arkansas. Many freed people lived in this town. The outbreak killed 62 people. Freedmen's Bureau doctors were able to stop the outbreak. They treated the sick people. They helped people find clean water. Without their help, many more people would have died.

## EDUCATION

The Freedmen's Bureau also built schools for black people. It had been illegal to teach enslaved people to read or write. Bureau schools gave freed people the opportunity to get an education.

The American Missionary Association (AMA) helped the bureau build schools. The AMA and other charity organizations recruited teachers to come to the South. They often paid the teachers' salaries and expenses.

## BUREAU TEACHERS

**Thousands of teachers came to the South in the 1860s and 1870s. Charity organizations recruited white and black teachers. The teachers taught in Freedmen's Bureau schools. Most were unmarried and well educated. Many came from middle-class homes in the North. Many white southerners did not welcome the teachers. Most slaveholders had believed that enslaved people should not be educated. Many former slaveholders still held this view of black people. Some southerners targeted the teachers. They burned down bureau schools. They attacked teachers.**

By 1870 the Freedmen's Bureau had created more than 4,300 schools for black students. Schools at the time were racially segregated. Black people were not allowed to attend the same schools as white people. Approximately 250,000 students attended bureau schools. The bureau recognized that education was key to black people's success. Bureau schools trained black people in many subjects. Some of these schools taught skills such as carpentry and machine repair. Black people could use these skills to start their own businesses.

Black people knew the importance of education too. Some raised money to start schools. By 1870 many black southerners had built their own schools. Support from the Freedmen's Bureau had helped them accomplish this.

## EXPLORE ONLINE

**Chapter Four discusses how the Freedmen's Bureau provided education to black people. The article at the website below talks about educational opportunities for black people in Georgia in the mid-1800s. The school system in Georgia was similar to others in the South. What information does the website give about this topic? How is the information from the website the same as the information in Chapter Four? What new information did you learn?**

FREEDMEN'S EDUCATION DURING RECONSTRUCTION
**abdocorelibrary.com/freedmens-bureau**

CHAPTER
# FIVE

# THE BUREAU'S LEGACY

The Freedmen's Bureau faced widespread opposition in the South. White hate groups targeted black people. The Ku Klux Klan (KKK) was the most well known among these groups. KKK members attacked and even killed black people. Because bureau agents aided black people, some white people also targeted them. Agents faced many threats. Some were killed. Still, the bureau continued its work.

In July 1868, Congress decided that the most of the bureau's duties would end on December 31 of that year. Its educational projects would continue until 1872.

**Some white southerners burned Freedmen's Bureau schools.**

## SUCCESSES AND FAILURES

Some historians say that the Freedmen's Bureau was a failure. The bureau was not given enough money or agents to accomplish all its goals. Its temporary status only allowed it to provide aid for a few years. Many of the changes the bureau made did not last. Courts continued to discriminate against black people. Few black people were able to buy land.

### BUREAU RECORDS

**Freedmen's Bureau officials kept detailed records. Historians study these records to learn more about black people's experiences after the Civil War. Today the records are available to the public. African Americans can search these records online to learn about their ancestry. This online database is called the Freedmen's Bureau Transcription Project.**

President Johnson's lack of support for the bureau was a major obstacle. Johnson opposed giving rights to former slaves. He vetoed bills to give the bureau money and more power. Many historians believe the bureau would have been able to accomplish more without Johnson's opposition.

Still, the bureau aided many people. By the end of 1868, it had issued more than 20 million food rations. It had treated thousands of sick people. It had opened many schools. The bureau also made a difference in labor conditions. It enforced free labor systems.

## PERSPECTIVES

### RACISM IN THE BUREAU

**Most bureau agents tried to be fair. But some did not look out for black people's interests. Some agents discouraged black people from attending political meetings. Other agents took bribes from planters. Chandra Manning is a history professor at Georgetown University. She said, "I think to really understand the Freedmen's Bureau, we'll do better if we can walk away from wanting it to be all good or all bad, or full of heroes, or full of racists who sold free people out."**

One of the bureau's greatest successes was its work within the court system. The bureau brought discrimination cases to federal courts. Federal courts

## UNEMPLOYMENT RATES

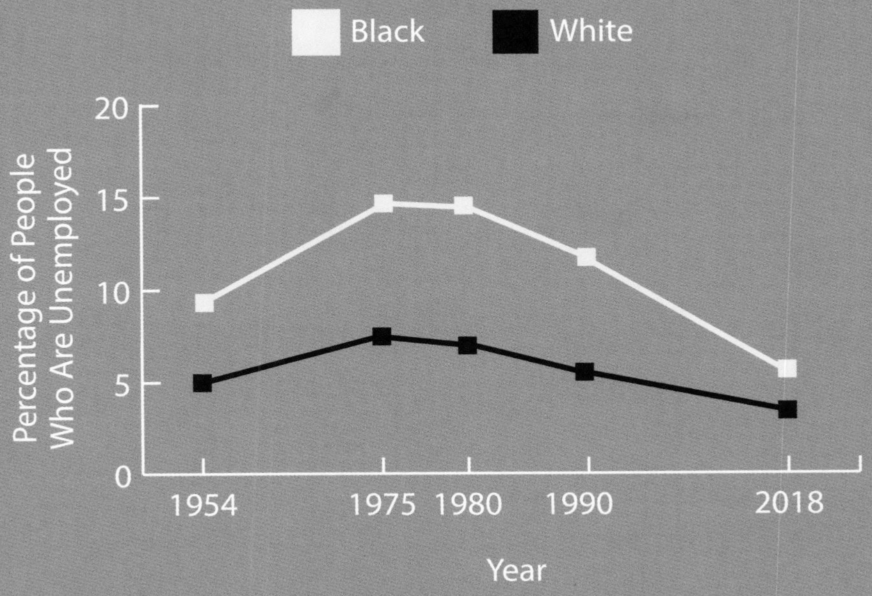


The Freedmen's Bureau helped former slaves find jobs. Few jobs were available to black people. Many were unemployed. The US Bureau of Labor Statistics began collecting data on unemployment by race in 1954. The above graph compares the black and white unemployment rates in certain years. Why do you think the black unemployment rate continues to be higher than the white unemployment rate? How do you think people could address this issue?

had not often interfered in state issues before. The bureau's defense of black people's rights is an important part of its legacy.

**African American law school students stand outside Howard University, a Freedmen's Bureau school, in the early 1900s.**

# FAST FACTS

- The Emancipation Proclamation went into effect on January 1, 1863. The Civil War ended in April 1865.
- The Freedmen's Bureau was created after the Civil War. President Andrew Johnson appointed General Oliver Howard to be the bureau's commissioner.
- The bureau fed thousands of newly freed slaves and white refugees. It also supervised labor contracts between black people and planters. It created special courts to hear legal cases between freedmen and planters.
- The bureau created more than 40 hospitals to treat freed people. It established 4,300 schools for black people.
- The bureau was meant to be temporary. It was only expected to exist for one year. But its services were extended until July 1868. Its educational projects continued until 1872.
- The bureau had limited funds. It faced widespread opposition. But it was able to give aid to many black people in a time of great need.

# STOP AND THINK

### Surprise Me

Chapter Four describes how the Freedmen's Bureau helped establish schools and hospitals for black people. After reading this book, what two or three facts about the Freedmen's Bureau did you find most surprising? Write a few sentences about each fact. Why did you find each fact surprising?

### Take a Stand

The Freedmen's Bureau faced a lot of opposition in the South. Some white hate groups targeted bureau agents. Do you think the federal government should have helped address this problem? Why or why not? How do you think this problem could have been addressed?

### Why Do I Care?

The Freedmen's Bureau was created more than 150 years ago. How might its legacy still live on today? How might your life or the lives of others be different if the Freedmen's Bureau hadn't been created?

# GLOSSARY

**abolish**
to officially end or do away with something

**amendment**
a change or an addition to an existing law

**discriminate**
to mistreat people because of their race or other perceived differences

**plantation**
a large farm where workers grow crops

**planter**
a person who owns a plantation

**racism**
the belief that certain people are better than others because of their race

**ratify**
to approve or confirm something

**refugee**
a person who flees to escape danger

**secede**
to separate and become independent from a nation

**segregate**
to separate people of different races or ethnic groups through separate schools and other public spaces

**veto**
to stop a bill from becoming a law

# ONLINE RESOURCES

To learn more about the Freedmen's Bureau, visit our free resource websites below.

**Core Library CONNECTION**
FREE! COMMON CORE MULTIMEDIA RESOURCES

Visit **abdocorelibrary.com** or scan this QR code for free Common Core resources for teachers and students, including vetted activities, multimedia, and booklinks, for deeper subject comprehension.

**Booklinks NONFICTION NETWORK**
FREE! ONLINE NONFICTION RESOURCES

Visit **abdobooklinks.com** or scan this QR code for free additional online weblinks for further learning. These links are routinely monitored and updated to provide the most current information available.

# LEARN MORE

Halls, Kelly Milner. *Life During the Civil War*. Minneapolis, MN: Abdo Publishing, 2015.

Rissman, Rebecca. *Slavery in the United States*. Minneapolis, MN: Abdo Publishing, 2015.

# ABOUT THE AUTHORS

## Duchess Harris, JD, PhD

Dr. Harris is a professor of American Studies at Macalester College and curator of the Duchess Harris Collection of ABDO books. She is also the coauthor of the titles in the collection, which features popular selections such as *Hidden Human Computers: The Black Women of NASA* and series including News Literacy and Being Female in America.

Before working with ABDO, Dr. Harris authored several other books on the topics of race, culture, and American history. She served as an associate editor for *Litigation News*, the American Bar Association Section of Litigation's quarterly flagship publication, and was the first editor in chief of *Law Raza*, an interactive online journal covering race and the law, published at William Mitchell College of Law. She has earned a PhD in American Studies from the University of Minnesota and a JD from William Mitchell College of Law.

## Bonnie Hinman

Bonnie Hinman has written more than 50 books for young people. She especially likes to write about American history. She lives in southwest Missouri near her children and five grandchildren. She lives with her husband, Bill.

# INDEX